1 MONTH OF
FREE
READING

at
www.ForgottenBooks.com

By purchasing this book you are eligible for one month membership to ForgottenBooks.com, giving you unlimited access to our entire collection of over 1,000,000 titles via our web site and mobile apps.

To claim your free month visit:
www.forgottenbooks.com/free904574

ISBN 978-0-265-88567-3
PIBN 10904574

VII.—THE DROIT DE BANALITÉ DURING THE FRENCH RÉGIME IN CANADA.

By W. BENNETT MUNRO, Ph. D.,

HARVARD UNIVERSITY.

THE DROIT DE BANALITÉ DURING THE FRENCH RÉGIME IN CANADA.

By W. Bennett Munro.

Among the many oppressive incidents which marked the land-tenure system of the old régime in France, not the least important were the "banal rights" (droits de banalité), or the privileges enjoyed by the seigniors of exclusively controlling certain of the instruments of production within their seigniories and of compelling the censitaires to make use of these mills, ovens, wine presses, slaughterhouses, and so on, to a fixed charge.

Whether in their origin these banal rights were the result of unlawful usurpations on the part of the seigniors—advantages wrested by strength from weakness—or whether they simply grew out of the mutual wants and interests of the parties concerned, has never been satisfactorily determined; their existence as legal rights was recognized, however, in only eleven out of the large number of French coutumes.[1] The other coutumes are either silent upon the whole subject of banalité, or speak of banal rights only as possible "servitudes" arising as the result of mutual agreements made between seignior and dependent.

Notwithstanding this, mention may be found of the droit de banalité in the etablessments and ordonnances as far back as the reign of Louis IX (1226–1270) and by the seventeenth century they had become—to use the words of Championnière[2]—"the most terrible abuse and the most general exaction of the whole seigniorial system."

Like most of the other seigniorial exactions, the banal rights varied very greatly, both in nature and extent, in different parts of France. The French Government, however,

---

[1] Henrion de Pansey, Dissertations Feodales (Paris, 1789), T. I., p. 175.
[2] De la Proprieté, etc., p. 552.

when it undertook to transplant to its North American pos-
sessions the system of seigniorial tenure, with all its incidents, endeavored to secure some degree of uniformity by
prescribing the Coutume de Paris as the colonial code. And
in thus relieving the colony of the legal confusion which
necessarily resulted from the existence of so many different
coutumes at home, the French authorities acted very pru-
dently. But their choice of a suitable coutume for colonial
use was in some respects less sagacious. The greater part of
the colonial settlers came from the northern provinces of
France,[1] Normandy contributing the largest share. Paris and
the surrounding districts contributed little beyond the administrative officials and the members of the religious orders.
Furthermore, the immigrants to the colony came, as a rule,
from the agricultural class and not from the industrial or
commercial, so that upon arrival in Canada they found themselves subject to a code of laws which was not only totally
unfamiliar to them, but also out of harmony with the needs
of an agricultural colony. This, nevertheless, was the coutume—framed for the use of an urban population—which the
French Crown saw fit to introduce, and all the relations of the
colonial seignior and censitaire were henceforth regulated
according to its provisions.

The Coutume de Paris, as revised in 1580, recognized the
enforcement of banal rights by the seigniors, but with two
important limitations regarding the rights as applied to mills
and ovens. These were:

(1) No seignior can compel his subjects to go to the oven or mill which
he pretends banal * * * if he have not a valid title * * * and no
title is reputed valid if it has not been executed more than twenty-five
years.[2].

(2) A windmill (moulin à vent) can not be banal, nor under this pre-
text can the neighboring millers be prevented from canvassing for grain
(chasser), if there be not a written title or acknowledgment as above.[3]

According to this custom, therefore, the rights of mill and
oven banality—which were the only ones ever enforced in
Canada—were not prescriptive, but contractual rights. They
could be exacted by the seignior only when they had been

[1] Sulte, Origin of the French Canadians (Ottawa, 1897), p. 7.
[2] Brodeau, Coutume de Paris, Art. 71.
[3] Ibid., Art. 72.

expressly stipulated for in the title deeds of his subgrants, and in no case could a windmill be deemed a basis for the enforcement of banal rights. As the former of these limitations did not appear in the Coutume de Paris before 1580, but was inserted during the course of the revision in that year, it would seem as if the policy of the French Government was to place more restrictions upon the exercise of the rights of banality by the seigniors.

In Canada, on the other hand, not only were these restrictions disregarded, but, as we shall find, the French Crown and its representatives took active measures to establish and enforce the banal obligations in all parts of the colony. And, paradoxical as it may appear, the chief burden of this enforcement fell not upon the censitaires, but upon the seigniors.

During the period of almost half a century (1627–1663), throughout which the colony was in the hands of the Company of One Hundred Associates, very few of the sixty-odd grants en fief were taken in hand by the grantees. The object of the company was, primarily, to fill its coffers with the profits of the fur trade, and the directors paid very little attention to the matter of colonial settlement or organization. On a few of the seigniories, however, mills were built and used by the somewhat sparse population, under what conditions of payment can not be definitely ascertained. In 1652 we find trace of the first official regulation concerning the management of the seigniorial mills in an ordinance of the governor, M. de Lauzon. This ordinance was, apparently, never enregistered, as no copy of it can be found, but mention is made of it some fifteen years later in an ordinance issued by the intendant and council reiterating its purport and ordering its enforcement. This later ordinance[1] (March 28, 1667) goes on to declare that—

Considering that it has been represented to us by the attorney-general that several abuses are being committed by the millers of this country with respect to the grinding of grain, and to remedy which it would seem fit to reiterate the ordinance made in 1652 by the late governor of this country, M. de Lauzon, and, reviewing the said ordinance, the council, adjudicating thereon, hath ordained and doth ordain that it shall have its full and entire force, saving the right of adding to it in future should necessity arise.

---

[1] Edits et Ordonnances concernant le Canada, II, p. 36.

The ordinance then proceeds to provide that "the damages suffered by tenants carrying their grain to be ground" at the seigniorial mills "shall be had from the owners of the said mills, saving to these the right of deducting the same from the wages of their paid millers." These appear to have been the first ordinances relative to the management of banal mills, but others were not long in following. On June 20 of the same year (1667) an ordinance [1] of the intendant and council was issued in response to a petition presented some few days previously on behalf of "most of the proprietors of mills in the colony," wherein it was stated "that the mills of this colony cost double or treble those of France, as well for their construction, maintenance, and repair as for the wages and board of the millers," in consequence of which the petitioners declare that they might with justice ask "that the toll be proportioned to the above expenses and consequently be fixed above the usual toll in France." Notwithstanding this the petitioning seigniors went on to say that they were satisfied with the current rate of toll and ask for the issue of an ordinance fixing this customary rate for general use in the colony.

In accordance with the prayer of this petition, the ordinance of June 20, 1667, ordered the rate of toll to be fixed at one-fourteenth of the grain ground. Furthermore, it empowered the Government officials "to go from time to time from place to place to gauge the measures used in the mills, and to find out generally what is going on," and declared that where seigniors had leased their mills the censitaires should have recourse for damages, "in the event of malversation by the millers," upon the lessee and not upon the proprietor. Finally, in order to guard both against fraud on the part of the miller and the preferring of groundless accusations by the censitaire, the ordinance required that "owners of grain taken to be ground should be held to have their grain weighed, in default of which their complaints should not be heard." This practice of administrative interference in the management of seigniorial mills was not peculiar to the colony; it had been common in France, where it was justified on the grounds of public policy.[2]

---

[1] Edits et ordonnances concernant le Canada, II, p. 39.

[2] Regarding this Henrion de Pansey observes (Dissertations Feodales. Paris, 1789, p. 215, sec. 19): "But above the authority of the seigniors there is an authority of a higher

In France the amount of toll exacted for the grinding of corn at the banal mills varied in different parts of the Kingdom. In the Coutume de Paris it was fixed at one-fourteenth, and the effect of the ordinance of 1667 was therefore simply to specifically apply this rate to the colony. The remuneration of the seigniorial mill owner, being fixed at a definite percentage of the grist, varied, obviously, with variations in the price of grain, which latter, especially during the closing period of the French régime, were very marked. During the period of thirty years from 1729 to 1759 the price of wheat ranged all the way from 2 francs to 10 francs per minot, or measure of about three French bushels.

But despite the assertions of the seigniors in the petition of 1667 that they would be satisfied with the usual rate of toll, there seem to have been some attempts on the part of certain of their number to exact more than the legal rate. In the lengthy code of " Police regulations," issued by the intendant some years later (1676), a clause was inserted[1] forbidding all millers from "causing more than one-fourteenth to be paid for the toll of grist." Likewise, the millers of each seigniory are forbidden to compete with one another (le chasseur les uns sur les autres), as e. g., by soliciting grist from the inhabitants of seigniories other than their own.

But the number of mills increased very slowly, owing, doubtless, to the poverty of the seigniors, most of whom could ill afford the means necessary to build the mills and to import from France the needed machinery. The stones were quarried in the colony; all else had to be imported. The toll received, except in the case of the more populous seigniories, often scarcely sufficed to pay the wages of a miller and the result was that in many of the seigniories no mills were erected. This state of affairs was soon brought to the notice of the French King, and the latter, in keeping with his usual zeal for the rapid development of the colony and in consonance with his unlimited faith in the efficacy of royal edicts as the general panacea for tardy industrial progress, at once set

order to which belongs all that can interest public policy, * * * and which has the right to restrict the liberty of each individual for the good of the greatest number. The mills intended to give the first preparations to the chief article of food must necessarily be subject to the inspection of this supreme authority, which has, then, the right not only to control them but to regulate their number."

[1] Ed. et Ord., II, 65–71, sec. 35.

about a reformation of the colonial milling industry.   In 1686 he issued an important arrêt,[1] one of the most important edicts concerning the droit de banalité in the colony.   After declaring that he has been informed "that most of the seigniors who are holders of fiefs in New France neglect to erect the banal mills necessary for the subsistence of the inhabitants of the country," and, "in order to remedy an evil so prejudicial to colonial welfare," he proceeded to ordain that "all seigniors who are holders of fiefs within the territory of New France should be bound to erect their banal mills therein within the space of one year after the publication of this decree," in default of their doing which "his majesty permits all individuals, of whatever condition and rank they may be, to erect such mills, granting to them in that respect the right of banality, and prohibits any persons from disturbing them in the right thereof."   This edict, the provisions of which were intended to stir up the unprogressive seigniors, was duly registered by the superior council at Quebec,[2] on October 21, 1686, and was ordered to be promulgated at the necessary and accustomed places.   Strange to say, this required publication did not take place till some twenty years later. During the period 1686–1707 the seigniors continued to build mills or not, as they found it profitable to do so or not to do so. In the latter case, however, they invariably took care to insert in their contracts of concession the obligation on the part of the grantees to carry their grain to the seigniorial mill "whenever such shall be erected within the seigniory."   The long delay in the publication of the arrêt of 1686 is, in all probability, correctly explained by M. Raudot, intendant of Canada, in a dispatch to the French minister, dated November 10, 1707.[3]

He writes:

I should think, My Lord, that it would be necessary * * * that the exclusive right of grinding should be preserved to the seigniors on condition of their building a mill on their seigniories within a year, failing in which their right should be forfeited, and the inhabitants would not be obliged when one was built to have their corn ground there; otherwise, My Lord, they will never be induced to erect mills, from the privation of

---

[1] Ed. et Ord., I, p. 255.

[2] Ibid., p. 256.

[3] Raudot à Pontchartrain, 10 November, 1707, Correspondance Générale (Canadian Archives), Vol. XXVI.

which the inhabitants suffer greatly, being unable, for want of means, to avail themselves of the favor which his majesty has granted them by permitting them to erect mills in case the seigniors do not do so.

The dispatch continues:

This was granted them in the year 1686 by an arrêt which was registered by the superior council of this country, but not having been sent to the subordinate jurisdictions to be promulgated, the inhabitants have not hitherto profited by this favor, and it is only since my arrival here that the decree has been published, the fact of its nonpublication having only come to my knowledge in the course of a lawsuit, recently determined, in which the arrêt was produced, but one of the parties was not able to take advantage of it because it had never been promulgated.

And he goes on to say:

.The fault can only be attributed to the Sieur d'Auteuil, whose duty as attorney-general is to transmit such decrees to the subordinate courts, but it was his interest as a seignior, as also that of some of the other councilors who are also seigniors, not to make known this decree.

Raudot proceeded, on the discovery of this nonpublication of the royal arrêt to issue an ordinance ordering its publication without delay.[1] From the foregoing may be seen plainly the desire of Louis XIV to make the droit de banalité obligatory in all parts of the colony, in the interest, however, not of the seignior, but of the habitant, together with the equally strong disinclination of many of the seigniors to conform to the royal will.

By the Coutume de Paris (article 71) no seignior was allowed to exact the droit de banalité from his dependents unless he had stipulated for such right in his deeds of concession. In the colony this limitation was not observed. Wherever a seigniorial mill was erected the censitaires were required to carry their grain thither to be ground whether this condition had been imposed upon them by their title deeds or not, and wherever the seignior met with refusal the aid of the intendant was invoked. For example, some of the censitaires of

---

[1] Ed. et Ord., II, 145-150. The orders of the French Government relative to colonial affairs were communicated to the officials of the colony in two ways: (1) By arrêts or edicts dispatched to the intendant, and registered in the records of the superior council at Quebec, which corresponded to the parliament of Paris in France. This council consisted of the governor, intendant, and bishops of the colony ex officio, together with certain other officials (generally drawn from the colonial population) appointed by the King. After registry these arrêts were published by being sent to the royal courts at Montreal, Quebec, and Three Rivers, to be read in open court; (2) By private instructions to the governor and intendant These were not enregistered, nor was any promulgation of their contents made.

Demaure in 1716 refused to avail themselves of the seigniorial mill on the ground that their title deeds contained no provision compelling them to do so. The seignior, François Aubert, brought the matter before the intendant who issued an ordinance[1] ordering the censitaires one and all to bear their grain to the banal mill under penalty of a fine, the ordinance "to be published at the door of the parish church of the seigniory upon the first Sunday or fast day so that it may be diregarded by none."

Again, as has been seen, according to the Coutume de Paris a windmill could not be made banal (article 72). This distinction between mills driven by water power and wind power, as regards seigniorial rights based thereon, was likewise soon removed in the colony by an ordinance of the intendant issued in July, 1675.[2] The immediate cause of the issue of this ordinance was the presentation to the superior council of a petition signed by one Charles Morin, miller of the seigniory of Demaure, praying that he be permitted to grind the grain of the censitaires resident within the neighboring seigniory of Dombourg, inasmuch as the mill of the latter seigniory was worked by wind power and consequently could not be included within the category of banal mills.

The council, after hearing in defense the lessee of the Dombourg mill, and after taking the opinion of the attorney-general on the matter, decided to "dismiss the demand of the said Morin and to ordain that all mills, whether they be water mills or windmills (soit a eau soit a vent), which the seigniors have built or will hereafter build in their seigniories shall be banal mills, and that their censitaires who shall be bound by their deeds to that effect shall carry their grain to such mills." Furthermore, this ordinance forbade the proprietors of mills to induce censitaires of other seignories to come to their mills under penalty of fine, together with the confiscation of the grain and the vehicles carrying it. The issue of this ordinance is but one out of the many instances which mark the constant attempt on the part of the central power to adapt the seigniorial system to the changed customs under which it had been established. Every seigniory did not possess an available water power, and to deny the extension of the banal right to windmills would have given most of the seigniors a valid

---

[1] Ed. et Ord., II, 448–449.   [2] Ibid. II, 62.

excuse for neglecting to build their mills whenever they found such a course profitable, and would have thus deprived the censitaires of what was a convenience rather than a burden. There was, however, one disadvantage concerning the wind-mill—the power was very unreliable. The habitants[1] br ing ing their grist to the seigniorial windmill often found it necessary to lose many valuable hours waiting for the breeze to blow. A clause in the aforementioned ordinance therefore provided that if the windmill of their own seigniory could not grind their grain within the space of forty-eight hours after it had been brought thither, the habitants should have full liberty to take their grist elsewhere.

It will be seen that by the early years of the eighteenth century the banal right in Canada had differentiated itself in three ways from that existent in France under the custom of Paris.

1. The right could be enforced by the seigniors even although they had not stipulated for it in their contracts of concession.

2. All mills, whether driven by wind power or water power, could be made the basis for the exercise and enforcement of the banality.

3. Any seignior who failed to build a mill within the limits of his seigniory within a given time lost all claim to the right, the latter becoming the property of anyone who was willing to proceed with the erection of the mill.

The arrêt of 1707 was not allowed, like many others of its kind, to become a dead letter. Within a few months after its publication the intendant showed that he was in earnest by pronouncing the. forfeiture of the right in the case of the seignior of Mille Isles.

"All the inhabitants of the seigniory of Mille Isles," the decree of forfeiture recites, "have caused the seignior Dupré,[2] proprietor of the said seigniory, to come before us that he may be ordered to build a mill for them, or, if he do not choose to do so, to consent that they should be allowed to build one for themselves, in which case they should be discharged from their banal obligation and allowed to utilize the right for their own benefit."[3] The seignior having admitted

[1] The French-Canadian peasant always spurned the terms censitaire or roturier. He invariably spoke of himself as "the habitant."

[2] This is probably a misprint for Dugué or Duguay, who was seignior at this time. (See Titrés des Seigneuries, I, p. 59.)

[3] Judgment of 14 June, 1707, Ed. et Ord., II, 427. In 1720 the arrêt of 1707 was ordered to be enregistered, published, and enforced in Acadia as well as in "Canada," Ed. et Ord., II, 157.

his inability to proceed with the erection of a mill, the judgment proceeded to "permit the said habitants to erect a mill in such part of the seigniory as they shall deem fit, and by so doing to be discharged from the obligation of banality to the seignior forever, being allowed to exact it for their own advantage." Here we have, therefore, under a seigniorial system, the somewhat unusual spectacle of a group of censitaires being permitted to exercise seigniorial rights over themselves.[1] In the same month a somewhat similar judgment was issued against the seignior of Varennes, while others followed from time to time during the course of the next few years. After Raudot's tenure of the intendancy had expired, however, the enforcement of the arrêt of 1707 became more lax, and there can be no doubt that many seigniors neither built their mills nor were deprived of their rights.

Subsequent intendants devoted their attention rather to the reformation of abuses which had sprung up in connection with seigniorial mills already in operation. In 1715 a somewhat lengthy code of regulations[2] was framed, providing among other things "that the owners of banal mills shall be held * * * to have scales and weights, stamped and marked to weigh the wheat which shall be carried there to be ground and the flour which shall be made therefrom." The judges of the royal courts were given power, when this regulation was found not to have been complied with, to have proper scales and weights put in and arranged at the seignior's expense.[3] These judges were, furthermore, instructed to examine the toll measure of each mill and "to have it made exact and stamped, prohibiting all millers from taking toll with any other measure than that which shall have been so stamped." Millers are enjoined to cut the weight of the grain, toll deducted, upon a tally, handing over to the habitants one duplicate half of this, in order that they may verify the weight of their flour when it is handed over to them. They are, finally, forbidden, under penalty "even of corporal chastisement," to wet the grain brought to them in order to have the flour thereof heavier.[4] In addition to this general code of regulations, ordinances were issued from time to time seeking to

---

[1] Cf. Ashley, Economic History, Vol. I, p. 37.   [3] Ibid., Art. 5.
[2] Ed. et Ord., II, 169.   [4] Ibid., Art. 9.

effect improvements in the machinery and management of particular mills, and from the very considerable number of these it would seem that the system of seigniorial flour making was not always wholly satisfactory. For example, in 1714 one of the habitants of the seigniory of Vincelotte, having been brought before the council on a charge of having "sent his grain to strange mills," urged in defense of his action that he had been obliged to take part of his grain elsewhere than to the mill of his own seigniory, because the latter was "no good;" that it "made very bad flour," and that "the miller who worked the mill gave too small return of flour for grain."[1] The council declared the defense of the habitant good, and ordered the seignior to have his mill improved—having done which his right would be enforced. From this decision the seignior made appeal to the king, but the latter confirmed the action of the council, adding that habitants should be allowed to have their grain ground elsewhere whenever the seigniorial mill should be "stopped in any manner and for any reason whatsoever."

In 1728 several inhabitants of the seigniory of Grondines set forth, in a petition to the superior council that "they are compelled to take their grain to the windmill of the seigniory, which is most grievous and prejudicial to them inasmuch as the stones only crack up the wheat, both because the mill has been absolutely ruined by the different persons who have run it heretofore, and because the Sieur Hamelin, who now runs it (Hamelin was himself the seignior of Grondines), not being a miller by trade, simply increases the defects in the flour. [2] As it was flour, and not cracked wheat, which the habitants wanted, they asked that experts should be appointed to examine the mill and to report the state of affairs to the council. The seignior being called on for his defense, declared that his mill was "in excellent order;" that while it was true that he was running—or trying to run—the mill himself, this was not his fault, his miller having been called out to do military service; that he was just about to secure the services of a competent flour maker and, finally, that he invited the appointment of experts who should satisfy themselves of the truth of his statements. The council, taking the seignior at his word, ordered a visit to the mill by a board of experts, with what result is not recorded.

[1] Titles and Documents, II, 224. [2] Ed. et Ord. III, 241.

In the same year the habitants of the seigniory of St. Anne
de la Pérade sent a delegation before the authorities at Quebec
to complain that the mill of that seigniory was "entirely out
of order;" that "the miller was not only a dishonest man, but
was known to the seignior as such," and that the mill was not
of sufficient capacity to grind out all the flour which was
required for the maintenance of the habitants and their fami-
lies.[1]   The inhabitants of the seigniory of Neuville were better provided for, since there were in the seigniory two banal
mills—one a windmill, the other a water-power affair.   This
double facility appears, however, to have availed them little,
for in 1733 they made complaint to the council that the former
seldom ran, and the latter turned out defective flour.   Furthermore, they declared that "when the windmill failed for wind
or the water-mill for water the seignior kept them hauling
their grain back and forward from one mill to the other as
often as three times."[2]

They asked, among other things, that the seignior be ordered
to keep a regular miller, who should live near the mill, and
that he should provide "stamped weights of iron instead of
stones, the weight whereof is not shown."   In this last request
is an interesting bit of evidence as to the general equipment
of the banal mills of the old régime.

Complaints were sometimes made that seigniorial mills had
been erected in places which the habitants found it difficult to
reach.   In one case the intendant ordered a seignior to have
his mill built on the riverside, where it could be reached by
boat, or else to have a road built up to it.[3]   In another case
the same official allowed certain habitants exemption from the
banal obligation until their seignior should have opened up a
passable road.[4]   In a country where seigniories extended, as
they frequently did, over from 200 to 500 square miles, the
difficulty of transporting the grain to the mill was often very
serious.   As to the choice of a mill site, the seignior was
unhampered.   If he saw fit to erect it upon land which had
been already granted to a habitant, he could obtain a decree
from the council reuniting this land to his demesne, the habitant being given the privilege of selecting a new concession
of similar extent from any portion of the ungranted lands of

[1] Ed. et Ord., II, 497.   [3] Ed. et Ord., II, 210.
[2] Tit. and Docs., II, 155.   [4] Perault's Extracts, p. 71.

the seigniory. In some cases decrees of this kind were granted.[1]

In response to repeated complaints that habitants were being put to much inconvenience by having to wait on windmills to start running during calm weather, an ordinance was issued in 1730 giving all persons liberty to take their grain to a water-power mill, if compelled to leave their grist unground at the seigniorial windmill for more than two days.[2] This provision, which was greatly appreciated by the habitants in general, was issued chiefly through the influence of Giles Hocquart, who with the exception of Jean Talon—the Colbert of New France—was perhaps the most public-spirited as well as the most energetic of the colonial intendants. Hocquart during the course of his régime rigidly obliged seigniors to keep their mills in good repair, going so far as to threaten them with entire deprivation of the banal right in the event of their failure to comply with his demands.[3]

In the course of one of his dispatches, Hocquart advised the French Government that the quality of the flour turned out by the banal mills would be materially improved if the grain were only properly cleaned before being ground, but that there were no fanning mills in the colony. The seigniors, in all probability, deemed it sufficient to build the mills and to run them for the most part at a loss, without providing subsidiary appliances. The French King, however, with his usual zeal for the development of colonial industry, promptly gratified the desire of the intendant by sending out, in 1732, six fanning mills at his own expense. On arrival in the colony, these were distributed, gratis, among six of the most important seignioral mills—those of the seigniories of Sault a la puce, Petit-Pre, Beauport, Point de Levy, St. Nicholas, and St. Famille—and an ordinance[4] was forthwith issued, compelling the owners of those mills "to have all the wheat of whatsoever quality sent to them passed and fanned before its conversion into flour." It was further ordered that the millers should take their toll merely upon the cleaned and fanned grain and not upon the whole, but that in compensation for this the millers should be allowed to exact 6 deniers per minot on the whole grist, in addition to the usual toll of

[1] Ed. et Ord., II, 466.

[2] Ibid., 340.

[3] Ibid., II, 519.

[4] Ibid., 352.

one-fourteenth. All "taillings" were to be given back to the habitant.

During the course of the next year five more fanning mills were sent out and distributed among the seignioral mills in the district of Montreal,[1] the King promising to keep up the good work but failing thereafter to do so. The seigniors themselves showed very little industrial enterprise at any time, and this may be accounted for partly by the comparative poverty of the greater portion of their number, and partly, too, by the fact that many of them were retired military and administrative officials with little taste for industrial life. Absenteeism, one of the curses of the seigniorial system in France, was never an evil in Canada, and the writer who declares that "the peasants looked upon their lords in the light of taxpayers wringing money out of labor to spend it in luxury in Quebec and Montreal"[2] has attributed to the colonial seigniorial system a feature which it fortunately never inherited from the motherland. The great majority of the Canadian seigniors shared the rough everyday life of their pioneer dependents—very frequently they numbered among their censitaires men better endowed with worldly goods than themselves—and the number of seigniors whose means permitted luxurious idleness in the towns could be counted upon the fingers of one hand.[3] In France, again, the seignior was almost invariably a member of the noblesse; in the colony this was rarely the case, with the result that there was no legal bar to his engaging in manual work, and the colonial prototype of the haughty seigneur who lounged in the corridors of Versailles might not infrequently be found crushing grain in his little mill on the banks of the St. Maurice.

The seigniorial mills were usually constructed of timber, but in not a few cases they were built of stone, many of the seigniors expressly reserving in the titles of their subgrants the right to take materials for this purpose from the conceded lands without compensation. In a few cases the habitants were obliged to render their *corvées* in preparing the materials and even in erecting the mills, but this practice was never sanctioned by the authorities. The stone mills were usually

---

[1] These were given one each to the mills of Lachine, Isle Jesus, and Isle St. Helene, and two to the mill of the seigniory of Terrebonne.

[2] Watson, Constitutional History of Canada, p. 12.

[3] C. F. Sulte, La Tenure Seigneuriale in Revue Canadienne (August, 1882).

loopholed in order to be available as places of refuge and
defense in the event of Indian attacks, and the mill of the
seigniory of St. Sulpice at Montreal was one of the chief
strongholds of the town. The religious orders were, in fact,
able to build much better mills upon their various seigniories
than were the individual lay seigniors, and these they almost
invariably fortified, for during the greater part of the period
of French possession no part of Canada was safe from an
Iroquois assault.

Three questions have been much mooted in regard to the
extent of the droit de banalité in the colony. The first of
these was as to whether all the grain produced by the censitaires was subject to the banal obligation, or only such portion
of it as was required for the consumption of the producer
and his family. Some of the seigniors took the former view,
but the authorities thought differently and ordinances were
refused to seigniors who wished thereby to compel habitants
to bring all their grain to the seigniorial mills. On the other
hand, the intendant never refused, in default of good reason
to the contrary, to enforce the obligation in regard to grain
used by the habitant and his family.[1] The action of the
authorities in this regard has been upheld by the most author-
itative writers upon the subject of French-Canadian civil
law,[2] and would seem to be borne out by the wording of the
long-suppressed arrêt of 1686, which speaks of the neglect of
the seigniors to build the banal mills "necessary for the subsistence of the inhabitants," a feature which might be taken
to show that in the opinion of the French Crown the primary
object of the system of banal mills in the colony was to insure
the grinding of grain for home consumption. The question,
however, was never of very great importance, for the habitants were generally able to produce but little grain more
than was sufficient for their own use. It was by no means an
uncommon occurrence to import flour from France for the
use of the urban population of the colony.

Then there was the more important question as to whether
the banal obligation extended to all grain intended by the
habitant for his own use, or the wheat alone. As to the extent of the right in France there is some difference of opinion

[1] Cf. Case of the Seignior of Champlain, Ed. et Ord., II, 452.
[2] Cugnet. Traité de la loi des fiefs, p. 36.

among writers.   Henrion de Pansey[1] affirms that it extended
not only to wheat, but to barley, buckwheat, and all other
grains.   Denizart, in his decisions,[2] quotes a judgment of the
parliament of Bretagne in which a seignior was sustained in
his claim that barley should be included within the category
of cereals subject to the droit de banalité.   Other authorities
of equal weight declare that the right usually extended to
wheat only.[3]   No doubt the extent of the obligation varied
in different parts of the country, but on the whole the general
weight of opinion seems to be in favor of the view that it
was properly applicable to wheat alone.[4]   In Canada, on the
contrary, the obligation was generally understood to have
been applicable to grain of all kinds.   The expression made
use of in the arrêts and ordinances was invariably "porter
moudre leur grains,"[5] and the term "grains" can scarcely be
construed to have meant cereals of any one kind.   The same
expression is used in the titles of lands granted en censive by
the Crown in the vicinity of Detroit, Mich.,[6] and it is also
the wording usually employed by the various seigniors in
their titles of concession.   In some few of the latter cases,
however, the expression "porter moudre leur bled" occurs,
in which case the intention would seem to have been to attach
the obligation to wheat alone.   These cases were very excep-
tional, and, in general, the fact that the intendant was apparently only once[7] called upon to decide the question in favor
of the extension would go to show that the extension of the
right to grain of all kinds was not opposed by the habitant.
Finally there was a question as to whether a censitaire purchasing grain outside the limits of the seigniory and having
it brought within was or was not bound to have it ground at
the seigniorial mill.   Henrion de Pansey, on this point, quotes
an arrêt de Gonesse, in which it is authoritively stated that
all grain, whether grown within or brought within a seigniory, was subject to the banal right.[8]   There is no colonial

[1] Dissertationes Feodales I, Vo. Banalité, p. 9.
[2] Nouveau Denizart, p. 648, sec. 5.
[3] Le Febre, III, 168, 173–175; Rousseau de la Combe, II, 67.
[4] Cf. Opinion of Judge Caron (Reports of the Special Seigniorial Abolition Court, 1854),
Vol. B, p. 38d.
[5] Cf. Arrêt of 1675, ordinances of 10th June, 1728, and 23d July, 1742, Ed. et Ord. Vol. II.
[6] Titres des Seigneuries, I, pp. 235, 258.
[7] Ed. et Ord, II, 323.
[8] Henrion de Pansey, op. cit., I, pp. 9–10.

arrêt or ordinance bearing directly on the point; but the
understanding seems to have been that when grain was both
purchased and ground without the seigniory, the flour might
be brought home and used without the necessity of any toll
being paid to the seignior within whose fief it was brought.
But where the grain was purchased outside the seigniory and
brought home unground, it ranked on the same footing as
grain grown within the seigniory. The general tendency
was to look on the right of banality as a personal right. It
was not because the grain had been grown within the seigniory that it was subject to the obligation, but rather because
the habitant owning it lived within the seigniorial jurisdic-
tion. Thus grain purchased within the limits of a seigniory
by a person without was subject to the banal obligation, not
in the seigniory within which the grain was bought, but in
the seigniory in which he was a censitaire.

The right of banality carried with it the right, not only to
prevent the erection of other than seigniorial mills within
the seigniory, but even to compel the demolition of such
after they had been erected. Instances are on record of the
enforcement of these latter rights by ordinances of the intendant, proceedings which were attended with considerable
hardship. For example, one of the inhabitants of the seigniory of Lauzon was, in 1698, given permission by the seignior
to erect a mill, there being no banal mill in operation.
Shortly afterwards the seigniory was sold and the new seignior
at once ordered the mill closed, and on the refusal of the
owner to comply, an intendant's ordinance was procured to
enforce compliance.[1] Similarly the brethren of the hospital
(Frères Charron) at Montreal had erected a small windmill to
supply their own wants. This mill was, however, within the
limits of the seigniory belonging to the Seminary of Sulpice,
and the latter applied for permission to have the mill demol-
ished. The intendant ordered this to be done in case the mill
should be found to be infringing upon the seigniorial rights
of the seminary.[2]

It will be seen, therefore, that on the whole the banal obligation did not in the period of the French régime bear very

[1] Ed. et Ord., II, 145.
[2] This arrêt is not printed. Its authenticity is vouched for by Chief Justice Sir L. H.
Lafontaine (in his judgment of the special court, 1854, p. 334).

heavily upon the habitant. In the majority of cases the seignior was the loser. With the passing of the colony into the hands of Great Britain, however, this state of affairs was somewhat changed. By the treaty of Paris the seigniors were guaranteed full possession of their ancient privileges, and with the great growth in population which succeeded the change of colonial ownership these rights, not the least important of which was the droit de banalité, became much more valuable. In very many of the seigniories the banal mill was no longer capable of doing all the work required and it became the custom of the seigniors to allow the habitants to take their grist elsewhere upon the payment of a fixed sum.[1] To this necessity of paying two tolls the habitants soon began to strenuously object, but the newly established English courts in the cases which came before them invariably upheld the claims of the seigniors. Prominent among the decisions in this regard was that given in the case of Monk v. Morris,[2] in which the court distinctly declared that the droit de banalité existed in full force under the new régime; that it was enforceable even without the possession of specific title; that it applied to grain of all kinds; that seigniors could compel the demolition of any nonseigniorial mills erected within the limits of their seigniories. The seigniors in these matters had custom on their side, and precedents in the eyes of the English judges were all-powerful. In the eyes of the French intendants of the old régime precedents had counted for almost nothing when the course marked out by them conflicted with what was deemed the general weal. The legal result of the conquest was thus to deprive the habitants of one of their chief sources of protection.

During the whole of the first half of the present century the habitants of French Canada kept clamoring for the abolition of the seigniorial system with its various incidents, of which the droit de banalité now formed one of the most objectionable, and in 1854 their ends were obtained by the passing of the "seigniorial tenures abolition act,"[3] by the terms of which all

---

[1] It is interesting to note that in England, where the droit de banalité existed to some extent for a considerable time, it was frequently the practice of the townsmen within seigniorial jurisdictions to obtain exemption from its exercise by the payment of a sum in commutation. In this, however, they were not always successful, as, e. g., the case of the men of St. Albans (Cunningham, Growth of English Industry and Commerce, Vol. I), who had not obtained exemption as late as 1381.

[2] 3 Lower Canada Reports, pp. 17 et seq.   [3] 18 Vict., 6, III.

lands held en fief, en arrière-fief, en censive, and en roturier were converted into free and common socage holdings, due compensation being awarded to the seigniors, partly in the form of constituted rents upon the land and partly in funds from the public treasury. The questions regarding the extent of rights for which the seigniors claimed compensation was referred to a special court composed of all the judges of the superior courts.[1] In regard to the right of banality this court decided that while, according to the custom of Paris, this obligation was a contractual and not a prescriptive one, the arrêt of 1686 had abrogated this rule and made the droit de banalité a general right incidental to all grants en fief. The court, moreover, decided that the banal right extended to grist mills alone and did not apply to works (usines) of other kinds; that it applied only to such grain as was used by the habitant; and that lands which had been granted within the seigniories en franc aleu[2] were not subject to the obligation. Seigniors who had erected and operated mills were adjudged entitled to compensation, but those who had not done so prior to 1854 were deemed by the court to have forfeited any right to indemnity. The act of 1854 provided that expert valuators should visit all the seigniories and should "estimate the probable decrease (if any) in the net yearly income of the seignior resulting from his loss of his right of banality,"[3] taking into account the foregoing conclusions of the court; the sum so estimated to be apportioned upon the granted lands of the seigniory in proportion to their extent. A large sum was also set aside from the public treasury for the reduction of the sums so apportioned.

Thus ended the droit de banalité in Canada. There was, however, another species of banal right which, though by no means as important in the economic history of New France, calls for a passing notice. This was the droit de fours banalité, or right of oven banality. By the Coutume de Paris[4] the rights of oven and mill banality had been placed upon a similar basis; that is, a seignior could compel his censitaires to carry their dough to the seigniorial oven to be baked only if he had

---

[1] Decisions des Tribunaux, 1854, Vol. A.
[2] Some few freehold grants had been made by seigniors.
[3] 18 Vict. C., 3, Sec. VI, par. 3.
[4] Art. 71.

expressly stipulated for this privilege in his title deeds of concession.   As far as I can ascertain there was only one banal
oven ever erected in Canada, viz, that of M. Amiot, seignior
of Vincelotte, but the obligation was inserted in many of the
title deeds.   In Raudot's dispatch of November 10, 1707, to
which reference has already been made, the writer speaks of
the right of oven banality as being one of the abuses of the
colonial seigniorial system.   He says:

The seigniors have also introduced in their grants the exclusive right
of baking or keeping an oven (fours banal), of which the inhabitants
can never avail themselves, because the habitations being at great dis-
tances from the seignior's house where this oven must be established (which
indeed could not be in a more convenient place for them wherever placed,
since the habitations are very distant from one another), they could not
possibly at all seasons carry their dough to it; in winter it would be frozen
before it got there.

He continues:

The seigniors, moreover, feel themselves so ill-grounded in claiming this
right because of its impossibility that they do not exact it now, but they
will at some future time make use of this stipulation to compel the
inhabitants either to submit to it or redeem themselves from it by means
of a large fine; in this way will the seigniors have acquired a right from
which the inhabitants derive no benefit.   This, my Lord, is what I call
getting a title to vex them afterwards.[1]

Replying to this dispatch, the French minister, M. de Pontchartrain, advised that "with respect to the privilege of baking in the seignioral oven, all that is to be done is to follow
and enforce the arrêt of 1686, by which that matter has been
settled."[2]   The minister was here in error, for the arrêt of
1686 had reference wholly to banal mills, and contained not a·
word about banal ovens.   It had simply ordered that seigniors
who claimed the right to erect banal mills should erect them
at once or lose the right.   The question of ovens had not yet
arisen.   This advice of the minister did not satisfy the colonial intendant, who, in reply, pointed out that what he wanted
was the entire suppression of the right of oven banality, the
impossibility of enforcing which, he declared, would become
apparent when it was considered that "the inhabitants would
have to carry their dough a distance of 2 or 3 leagues in the
depth of winter."

[1] Raudot á Pontchartrain, 10th November, 1707; Correspondénce Génerale, Vol. XXVI.
[2] Pontchartrain á Raudot, 13th June, 1708, Seigniorial Documents (1854), p. 9.

He says:

It is a right which must be suppressed, because the inhabitants can derive no benefit from it, and the seigniors have established or wish to establish it only to oblige them to redeem themselves from it by condescending to pay in future some heavy charge. It is not so with the banal mills, the latter being always a benefit to the inhabitants who have not the means of erecting mills themselves, whereas the banal oven is a disadvantage, there being not one of them who has not an oven in his own house and as much wood as he wants to heat it.[1]

This correspondence is interesting as showing the valuable services rendered by the colonial intendants in the way of affording protection against unjust seigniorial exactions, a feature which was often sadly lacking in the conduct of the provincial intendants at home. It serves, further, to show that in the colony seigniorial rights were viewed by the authorities as resting upon a much more nearly utilitarian basis than in France.

The forebodings of the zealous intendant were, however, not well founded, for, with the exception of the single case given, the seigniors do not appear to have exacted either the right of oven banality or a money payment in its stead.

In France the seignior enjoyed the right to compel his censitaires to have their grapes pressed in the seigniorial wine press, and this privilege, especially in the southern part of France, was a very remunerative one. But in the colony there were no grapes and consequently no wine presses, seigniorial or otherwise.

It has been the practice of almost all writers on the history of Canada during the French régime to look upon the seigniorial system as one of the chief causes of tardy colonial development, and the action of the French Government in regard to the establishment of seigniorial mills has come in for especial criticism.[2] One writer goes to the other extreme, declaring that the banal right remained "almost a dead letter;"[3] but the fact is, as I have endeavored to show, that the French Government and its colonial representatives sought to develop the system of banal mills in the interests of the poorer habitants and not in the interests of the seigniorial proprietors. From the fact that royal edicts were found

[1] Raudot á Pontchartrain, October 18, 1708; Corr. Gén., Vol. XXVII.
[2] Cf. Parkman, Old Régime, p. 300–301.
[3] Goldwin Smith, Canada and the Canadian Question, p. 72.

necessary to force the seigniors to avail themselves of their privilege. it is very probable that during the greater part of the French régime there would have been no mills at all had the milling interest been left to private enterprise. Profit was to be found not in agriculture nor the manufacture of the products of agriculture, but in the fur trade, and the French Government must, in all justice, be given the credit of having realized that, so long as that was the case, the habitants must be given all possible facilities for turning their agricultural products to account with the least possible expense to themselves. So long as the population was sparse the system of banal grinding was, to the habitants, convenient and inexpensive. The burden fell upon the seigniors and they, though by no means opulent as a class, were after all best able to bear it.

De Tocqueville has aptly remarked that the physiognomy of a government may be best judged in its colonies:

When I wish to study the spirit and faults of the administration of Louis XIV, I must go to Canada. Its deformity is there seen as through a microscope.

As regards many features of the administration of Canada during the old régime this remark is undoubtedly true, but as regards the respective attitudes of the Government toward the exercise of the *droit de banalité* in Old and in New France, a striking exception to De Tocqueville's generalization makes itself apparent.

Lightning Source UK Ltd.
Milton Keynes UK
UKHW022203021218
333278UK00006B/692/P